D1191776

What Kind of Bird Are You?

Maxine Cooper Provost

GLADBROOK PUBLISHING COMPANY
New Canaan, Connecticut
Palm Desert, California

Copyright © 1987 by Maxine Cooper Provost

All rights reserved. No part of this book may be reproduced or transmitted in any form or by any means, except in connection with a review, without permission in writing from the publisher.

Communication with the author or publisher should be addressed to Gladbrook Publishing Company, 92 Valley Road, New Canaan, Connecticut 06840.

Printed in the United States of America

Smyth-sewn casebound

ISBN 0-9617640-0-7

Dedicated With Love and Respect . . .

To my parents, deceased, who provided a
wholesome environment in which to find myself,
and then gave me the freedom to spread my
wings. And . . .

To each of you who feels blessed because
you know that self-esteem and a sense of
responsibility light the path to personal
happiness and harmony with others.

Gratefully Acknowledging . . .

The comments and suggestions from family and friends, and their friends, who very generously gave their time to read and criticize the manuscript in various stages of development. To each of you, my sincere thanks.

This book is a sojourn...

. . . a sojourn for lighthearted souls who wish to smile as they take a look at themselves, and perhaps pick up a few seeds of insight into others.

The author's perceptions of people are based, not on scientific research, but on years of observing people "be themselves," then mentally filing them under certain types of personalities.

Brought forth now, each type described is a blending of similar personalities, not any particular individual. However, it is entirely possible that each individual reader will discover a type that is "just like me." Everyone seems to fit into one category or another.

CONTENTS

What kind of bird are you?   11
Of course, you have BITs   13
U Bs   14
BREEZ—the frank, outgoing optimist   15
FLASH—the caring, loyal fireball   19
WOE—the sensitive, many-mooded worrier   23
PRANCE—the magnanimous, capable, proud ego   27
Let's talk about specialness   32
PONDER—the creative, compassionate dreamer   35
JETT—the ingenious, dynamic doer   39
STEDDY—the patient, reliable, solid citizen   43
PLUME—the modest, meticulous charmer   47
Understanding others better   52
BOOM—the impulsive, independent, big boss   55
RIPPLE—the diplomatic, happy talker   59
EMBER—the shy, disciplined achiever   63
YAZOO—the inventive, absentminded rebel   67
Shining up your specialness   72
Good-bye   76
Birds are special too   78
Index   79
About the author   82

What Kind of Bird Are You?

No matter what your age, you may be somewhat of a stranger to yourself.

Well, you are about to get better acquainted because you will come to know your BITs. Oh yes, you do have BITs!

Sage will explain.....

SAGE
Our Guide

Of course, you have BITS!

You have as much chance of losing your BITs as of sitting in your own lap.

BITs are your Built-in Traits, your born-in qualities. You can shape them, you can fake them, berate them, even hate them, but you cannot escape them. The wise bird gets to know and understand them! For good reason. Understanding your BITs helps reveal the specialness of you and leads to feel-good relationships, including the most important one of all—you with you.

Come with Sage . . . .

U Bs

As you compare yourself and others to the birds, you will note that some have similar traits. Yet each is original...truly a U B.

Now, get that quizzical look off your face! Don't you know that a U B is a Unique Bird? Of course. Now don't you forget it!

So, read on. See how many of the birds are in YOUR world, and see if others agree when you know the answer to—WHAT KIND OF BIRD ARE YOU?

Smile! You simply
can't resist it
when you meet BREEZ......

BREEZ

sparkles with fun-loving spirit

Some U Bs are delightful charmers. Some are quiet thinkers or busy doers. Others are dreary pessimists . . .

Well, say "hello" to Breez—the amiable, likeable, gregarious optimist. Just look at that mile-wide smile. Breez's entire being exudes a high-spirited friendliness. When Breez talks, arms fling wide to emphasize a point. But wait. Did you hear what Breez just said?

"Those shoes really look good on you. They make your big feet look a little smaller."

You heard right. Breez is frankness in a bottle. With tactlessness for a stopper. But don't ruffle your feathers. Breez means no harm. It is simply a BIT—a Built-In Trait, remember! Breez sees things as they really are and blurts it out.

Take note of something else. Breez tends to be clumsy. Stumbles easily over nothing, such as an ordinary threshold. So, when Breez picks on *your* feet, realize it is unconscious self-criticism for awkward footwork. All of us birds are inclined to criticize others for shortcomings in ourselves. Besides, five minutes from now Breez most likely will be flattering you. That's Breez.

At the core of this bird's happy-go-lucky buoyancy is an incredible optimism. Some call it foolish optimism. It causes Breez to rush into "sure things," which could be as minor as making a bet on the local team or as major as following a hot tip on the stock market. What if the "sure thing" fizzles? Breez forgets fast, then leaps again, without looking, into the next big opportunity. Of course, Breez does have an occasional fling with Lady Luck—probably that BIT of optimism paying off!

Breez ignores advice. There are times it would be better to listen, but independence flares high in this bird's being. So do self-confidence and a touch of reckless daring; fortunately, these BITs are fortified with intelligence and versatility. All forged together, they cause Breez to explore the unknown, to jump at a challenge. You may see Breez doing flip-flops and circle 8's in the sky, trying to reach Cloud 9, and from your vantage point you know it is impossible. Nevertheless, save your breath. In due time Breez will land on Cloud 4 and shriek with delight, "Come on over to Cloud 4. It's the Shangri-la of the sky. Full of fun! Forget Cloud 9." Breez loves the unexpected, the spontaneous. Will Breez ever grow up?

Breez's happy, carefree spirit does have its negative aspects. Breez is restless, dislikes details and is forever misplacing something, especially keys. Breez detests waiting for anything or anybody, yet thinks nothing of making others wait, particularly when it involves one of Breez's own big promises.

If Breez cannot deliver, the attitude is an indifferent "so what." When pressed,

BREEZ
The Optimist

BREEZ

Breez turns on the charm and cleverly seeks sympathy or makes you feel dumb for asking. "It was your decision. You knew it was a long shot. . . . We might have made a bundle!" If tolerance is not one of your stronger virtues, you may accuse Breez of gross exaggeration or phoniness, irresponsibility, lack of discipline or simple carelessness. Breez could be guilty of any of these frailties if they are not firmly controlled. So, the next time Breez tries to entice you with a "big winner," consider it carefully. Remember that Breez is a born promoter.

Whether you work or play or live with Breez, you would be wise NOT to try to mend Breez's ways, if you want a harmonious relationship. Breez loves to be free—to go, to be, to do as Breez wishes. Breez hates commands, hates regimentation, hates confinement—BITs that are easier to live with when you understand them. And perhaps these BITs are the reason the Breezes of the world are often hard to catch in marriage.

Breez loves—yes, dearly loves—animals. And Breez loves travel and entertainment. They don't have to be "biggies." They can be as simple as a trip to the movies, or a visit with friends across town. A flirtatious, fun-loving soul, Breez finds great joy in socializing. "Come on over," or "let's meet at our usual spot" are common beckonings from Breez. However, it is more likely with friends than family, perhaps to avoid emotional ties which might make demands on Breez's freedom.

Whoever you are—family or friend—just enjoy Breez. After all, is life worth living if you can't have a little fun?

Do you see yourself in Breez—the frank, outgoing optimist?

A summary of Breez's BITs:
Amiable and gregarious; frank, at times thoughtlessly frank and tactless; very optimistic; leaps without looking; prone to exaggerate; versatile; restless; *impatient; independent; self-confident; fun-loving and spirited; hates regimentation; never seems to grow up; likes challenges, likes to be free; makes friends easily.*

18

Want a little excitement?
Chances are good you will
get it with Flash. . . . .

FLASH
The Fireball

20

FLASH
emotes at the drop of a feather

Run for cover! Hands tight to the ears! Unless, of course, you are making a study of anger in action. In that case, feast your eyes and ears on Flash, smack-dab in the middle of reacting to an insult. Nobody can attack the integrity of Flash's best friend and get away with it! If you have witnessed Flash's outpouring of wrath before, you know it has the explosive qualities of a cyclone rip-roaring along a warpath.

No need, though, to bemoan this U B's fiery BITs. Flash seems to enjoy the rampage, not for the commotion or attention, but for the release of inner passions and pressures.

Flash, you see, is a very intense, emotional being who keeps turbulent inner feelings under tight control. Until something triggers that ton of TNT. It could be an insult, ridicule, an injustice, immorality, jealousy or a pet peeve. Then Flash blows! Wow!

However, neither calamity nor dreadful hardship does it. If there's a serious family illness, dire financial problems or other adversity, Flash draws from a deep well of courage and endures, endures. But these sterling BITs remain hidden under normal circumstances. Herein lies a key to understanding Flash.

Everyone has a dual nature, traits that appear contradictory. Because Flash feels and expresses so profoundly, the duality reveals itself more readily. For example, after a thunderous outburst, great calm and composure. Or, despite flare-ups of suspicion and jealousy, great love and dedication to family and friends.

As a friend, Flash is pure gold. Loyal through thick and thin, and THERE when needed. Others may call to ask, "What can I do?" Flash arrives on your doorstep to give you help and comfort.

Yet, despite that openness of affection and friendship, you sense that Flash has a special need for privacy. There seems to be a part that remains hidden, a secret self reserved just for Flash. It creates an intriguing mystique. And adding to the mystery is Flash's uncanny ability to "read" people. Few, if any, can deceive Flash. A handy BIT, indeed!

If you have someone close to you who resembles Flash, you will never gripe that life is dull. The Flashes of the world are vibrant, magnetic, lively and passionate with a capital P. Yes, passionate in romance but also in everyday happenings. The merchandise arrived too late . . . the car broke down. Flash always reacts with BIG emotion. If that gush of exasperation, frustration, or whatever, sometimes gives you a feeling of being consumed, shrug it off. See it for what it is, not a tirade at you personally. Everyone tends to perceive things in relation to oneself, rather than the actual external factors. Remember, Flash cannot be lukewarm about anything. It is Flash's nature to emote. Enjoy the show!

Ooops! Wait a minute! There is a time you will NOT enjoy it—when you are the prime target of attack. If you happen to give Flash cause to throw a jealous fit—flirting with that new knock-out in the neighborhood could do it—watch out. Even after the fireball's big blast and apologies from you, this U B simply finds it hard to forgive. Not only that, Flash finds ways to get even with you and, for good measure, gives you the who-needs-you punishment. A negative BIT, to be sure, but don't forget, you asked for it. It is all part of the "getting along" game—becoming aware of each other's shortcomings and striving to understand them, and helping to strengthen each other's virtues.

Flash has many virtues—honesty, kindness, remarkable determination, perseverance. On the job, for example, Flash can sit tight and watch others move ahead to better assignments. Does Flash gripe? No. Flash searches out the secret to those promotions. Then, with smiling self-assurance and perfect calmness, works diligently and maneuvers when necessary to win the desired step up the ladder. No hurry. No fuss. But shrewdness? Yes. Resourcefulness? Yes. Tenacity? Definitely. And loyalty too. Flash never forgets who signs the paycheck. Lucky is the boss who hires this smart, well-motivated worker!

And lucky are you if you have a Flash in or near your nest. Nothing is ever drab or boring. With Flash you are riding high, with colors flying. You're riding a rainbow through life! Hold on tight!

Do you have some of the qualities of Flash—the caring, loyal fireball?

A summary of Flash's BITS:
Strong, intense feelings; easily excited; unduly emotional; vibrant with magnetic charm; cool composure; hot-tempered; possessive; affectionate, caring and loyal; dedicated, courageous and hard-working; secretive; jealous and suspicious; revengeful and unforgiving; persistent, determined, resourceful; self-assured; "reads" others well.

Do you worry?
Are you touchy?
Do you hate criticism?
Well, match your anxieties
with those of the next U B...

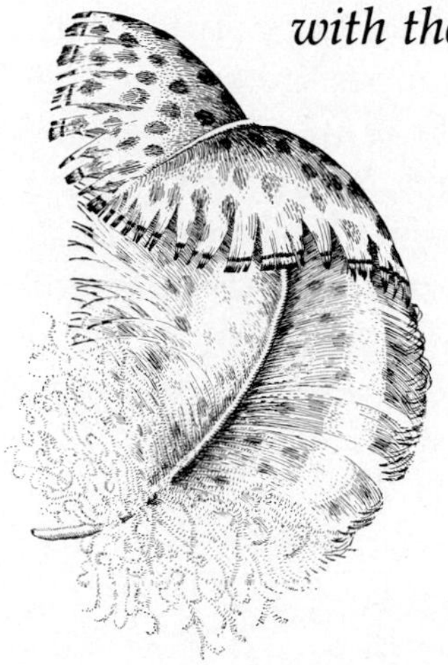

WOE

moans this hour and laughs the next

Poor Woe! Life is not a feeder full of sunflower seeds for this Unique Bird. It is just one disaster after another, or so it seems to Woe. Listen to the latest sad saga—

"This morning I had to stand in the pouring rain, waiting for my bus. Naturally it was late on a nasty day. Now I've caught cold. When I got to work, my boss was in a bad mood and demanded I finish a rush job. That made me miss lunch with my mother. Now I've got a headache."

Woe could win top honors in any "poor me" contest. All sorts of worries tug at Woe —money and job pressures, health anxieties, family differences, concern over Mother's living alone, plus a horrible feeling of inadequacy and haunting fear that "nobody loves me."

Indeed, both family and friends *do* love Woe. But there are others who deliberately shy away from nervous worry-birds with pessimistic imaginings. They seem to see only the somber face, perhaps because of insecurities within themselves or a simple lack of tolerance. Actually, Woe has many "faces" other than the doleful one, and that is what makes this U B so interesting as a friend or loved one.

If you happen to meet while shopping, Woe can be affable, eager to amuse you with the latest joke. Woe has a natural, rich sense of humor and a flair for telling one funny story after another. Woe loves to tell them, just to you or a roomful of people. That is the happy face of Woe. A delight!

But the next time you meet, perhaps a pop-in visit at Woe's home, Woe might be groaning over some setback. It could be financial, for Woe is thrifty and has a shrewd sense of the dollar. You feel as though you must change the subject, quick, to escape the quicksand of those negative moans. Woe does know that dwelling on misfortune adds to one's misery, that one must put the "gloomies" out of mind and doggedly turn to happy thoughts. But Woe is still working on that discipline. It comes easier to some than to others.

Another time you might find Woe quiet and pensive, the perfect mood for strolling through the park. Woe loves outdoor beauty and will notice little miracles of nature that escape the less sensitive. Woe will ask you to look into the very center of a flower, pointing out the glorious mixture of colors and the fragile filament of the stamen. Woe also can be the perfect companion to discuss the arts, the latest book or play. Woe's keen aesthetic senses detect subtle meanings and wider perspectives—rich conversation that nourishes the soul!

But then again, you can be chatting with Woe and snap, bang! Woe suddenly bristles with irritation. What happened?

WOE
The Worrier

25

WOE

You probably said something that appeared to be criticism, though that was not your intent. You may feel like barking back, or assuming a to-heck-with-you attitude, but if you care about this bird, try some gentle understanding. Remember that Woe is not snapping at you personally, but rebelling at some inner frustration. Woe suffers from an ever present sense of insecurity. This persistent BIT causes Woe to need more affection, more reassuring love, more "mothering" than most of us. But the rewards are worth it!

Woe has many positive BITs that compensate well for those occasional verbal whacks and pessimistic wails—quiet charm, sincerity, modesty, softheartedness, gentleness. But do not think Woe a wishy-washy pushover because of those tender qualities and inner undulating insecurities. Woe knows what Woe wants!

Probably most of all, Woe wants to love and protect dear ones, even if it means making sacrifices for them. If a cash crunch arises, Woe takes on extra work without flinching. Or if an ongoing problem becomes critical—perhaps a family member's social drinking now borders on alcoholism—Woe moves with caution, seeks authoritative help and enlists the support of those who are close. Though worry looms large, Woe perseveres till the problem is under control. This many-mooded U B can be a citadel of strength in trying times!

Woe also can be clever and shrewd in accomplishing a goal, but not at someone else's expense. "Lasting good never comes through loss to others," says Woe.

If you have a Woe in your flock, realize you have several friends all rolled into one with this Unique Bird. Know that no matter what the mood, Woe needs you, really needs you to help overcome those inner fears. Woe needs your special words of cheer and comfort, your reassuring love and understanding. Always. But don't we all thrive on being needed? Don't we gain through giving? Of course!

Do you feel akin to Woe—the sensitive, many-mooded worrier?

Summary of Woe's BITs:
Active imagination, sensitive, artistic; fretful, worrisome, moody; insecure, touchy and suddenly irritable; modest, sincere and serious; gentle and charming; pessimistic; inclined to self-pity; protective of loved ones; cautious, shrewd, thrifty and tenacious; good sense of humor; softhearted and sentimental; loves nature's beauty.

Atten-shun!
Stand erect.
Hold your head high.
And be sure to salute
the next, important U B.....

PRANCE
The Proud Ego

28

PRANCE
rules a private kingdom, or thinks so

It is very obvious! This Unique Bird is stuffed, absolutely stuffed, with self-importance.

Just who is this self-satisfied U B? It is Prance, the majestic one who stands tall, who regally scrutinizes a room upon entering, who walks—no, glides—with great dignity. The commanding presence of this bird gives you the feeling that Prance *is* ruling a private kingdom. And when you step inside the walls, you had better be filled with respect.

Therein lies one of the secrets of getting along with a proud, egotistical bird. Be respectful in even the smallest "little nothings" of daily living. Take a casual conversation, for example. When you disagree with Prance, be a smoothie and do it with a complimentary lead-in, such as "You seem so knowledgeable on the subject, but have you thought about it from this angle—" instead of a deflating knocker like "You don't know what you're talking about."

Remember, Prance types are born with feelings of superiority. So it is not really a matter of catering to them. It is you, very skillful in human relationships, being alert to the type of bird you are dealing with and knowing which technique to use to foster friendship and harmony.

If you have a Prance or two in your life, you may have discovered another secret in "handling" them. They love praise, considerably more than most of us. The praise you give may be pure flattery, and you may conceal a snicker in your sleeve at the transparency of it, but just watch. These birds luxuriate in it. "Of course!" declares Prance. "Praise is an elixir for body and soul." Thankfully, it is easy to laud these conceited U Bs, for they have warm, engaging personalities and vivacious, sexy charm. They have a flair for the dramatic and are full of fun and enthusiasm. And they reciprocate. They pay YOU effusive compliments, especially with others present. It is part of their grandiose approach to everything.

However, their grand style does not include a sensitivity to the feelings of others in day-to-day living. These birds are so engrossed in themselves they seldom note how others look or feel. If you happen to live with a Prance, the following may be familiar. You have come home exhausted. You thought your fatigue was obvious, but not to Prance. Before you know what is happening, Prance invites the neighbors for an impromptu evening of bridge. A malicious move? Revengeful? Not at all. The Big Ego is never cruel or unkind, but just following a whim of the moment—a privilege of rulers! But the diversion of bridge did ease your fatigue. Perhaps Prance was thinking of you after all. And you do respect the take-charge qualities in your mate.

These management abilities are a boon in community affairs, to say nothing of their value in a career. If your group is planning a fund-raising affair, put Prance in charge. This stately U B loves parties and has a great sense of showmanship. But, more important, Prance is a fantastic organizer whose enthusiasm is contagious. This born leader's knack of delegating jobs to the right people will make your event the happiest, most spectacular success of all time.

If emergencies arise along the way, do not worry. Despite wild exclamations about the horrendous crisis, Prance will pitch in with crackling energy and masterfully untangle the mess. Just make sure everyone knows it is Prance who is in command. In fact, right at the outset, give Prance an important sounding title. This U B delights in the dignity and authority of a title. It also will help avoid possible confrontations with the master sergeants in the group. Once provoked, Prance can be pompous, impulsively tactless, intolerant, condescending, even savagely rude. Negative BITs dramatically displayed, of course.

When the event is over, be lavish in your praise and appreciation of Prance's magnificent work. Better yet, express your plaudits in front of the crowd. Prance loves applause!

Prance also loves to splurge. Grand gestures of generosity are a firm fixture among this U B's BITs. Prance emphatically declares that giving to others brings good to you. Prance thinks nothing of treating family or friends to a "night on the town." There are those who say, "Prance is showing off again," but others with a mite more insight accept it with gratitude and graciously enjoy, enjoy.

Do you have a Prance in your life? If not, you are deprived! Start searching. Everyone needs a touch of the splendor, the drama, the pizzazz that only this noble U B can provide. Hail to the Prances!

Could you be a twin of Prance—the magnanimous, capable, proud ego?

A summary of Prance's BITs:
Vivacious, enthusiastic; affectionate; over-sized ego, feels superior; condescending, pompous, rude, tactless when provoked; intolerant and opinionated; energetic, responsible, a good organizer; delegates work well; stirs others to action; a show-off; a weakness for flattery; loves excitement; a flair for showmanship and drama.

30

What kind of bird are you?

You may or may not be an
optimist
fireball
worrier, or
proud ego
but
you are SPECIAL!

Sage

*L*et's talk about specialness

Woe

Prance

WOE: I don't know my specialness. I've never thought about it.

SAGE: A lot of us haven't, Woe. We simply *are* what we are.

PRANCE: Well, I know *my* specialness. Everybody should! When you know your good qualities, you can hold your head high and feel good about yourself.

SAGE: That's healthy self-esteem. It helps you accomplish goals and meet problems head-on.

WOE: With all my problems I'll never find my specialness.

SAGE: A pessimistic outlook is a frailty, Woe. But frailties can add to your specialness if you approach them in a positive, do-something way. They are really opportunities to grow emotionally and spiritually.

FLASH: Frailties are "uglies"! I detest mine! But I'm working on them.

BREEZ: I don't even think about mine. I guess I let my "uglies" just "flap in the wind."

FLASH: I think we all should *try* to overcome our faults, not just ignore them.

SAGE: Most of us resist changing our ways. We make excuses, and we feel a sense of comfort and security in the way we are, even if it's a bad trait causing irritation to ourselves or others. It takes real determination to correct our faults.

PRANCE: Think of yourself as flexible, like a ball of putty. That's what I do. When I've been disgustingly rude to someone, I picture myself reshaping that putty, squeezing the rudeness right out of me. It has cut back on my rudeness, but I must admit, I've got more squeezing to do.

SAGE: A positive approach, Prance! Of course, we're all evolving and changing ever so slightly every day, without even trying or being aware of it. The people and events that touch our lives have a way of making us think and feel in a little different way, see from a slightly new perspective. No one ever stays exactly the same.

FLASH: If only we could program ourselves like a computer!

SAGE: Actually, we've all been programmed since birth—by our parents, our teachers, our religious leaders, by our peers, our culture. As adults, we must take charge and program ourselves.

WOE: I'd like to push the computer "escape" key on all my nasty traits, like being deliberately unkind to myself. Sometimes I trip myself up as though I'd swallowed a self-destruct pill. It's really annoying.

SAGE: But Woe, you're *aware* of what you're doing to yourself. That's half the battle. Use the computer idea like Prance uses the putty. Hit the "escape" key when that unwanted thought or habit appears. Replace it with a trait you admire.

PRANCE: Then praise yourself for your achievement. I always do.

SAGE: But some of us must watch that we aren't too generous with self-praise. Even a good quality in excess becomes undesirable. Others of us need to give ourselves more praise to help build or reaffirm our self-esteem. It's good to hear praise from others, but the best recognition comes from your own self. *You* are your closest friend.

BREEZ: Now, that idea is new to me. I like it! I think I'll take myself out and celebrate.

PRANCE: Everybody in the whole, wide world knows I'm a good friend of me, but I've never celebrated it. I'll go with you.

FLASH: You two are for the birds!

SAGE: Having fun is part of their specialness. We all need lightness and humor, and some good times.

Breez

Flash

WOE:	Would you explain exactly what you mean by specialness?
SAGE:	It's the sum total of *you*, your uniqueness. It's how you think, see, hear and feel. How you talk, act, dream and love. It's what your attitudes are, what you care about, what you devote your energies to, what your priorities are. It's how you deal with your problems, how you adjust to life's tragedies and to life's triumphs. Your specialness is how you relate to those dear to you and how you relate to all the others. How you handle and understand yourself. It's all your qualities that make you different from everyone else. It is YOU, a unique being like no other.
WOE:	I'm beginning to feel special!
SAGE:	And what about YOU? Do you feel special? Are you glad to be *you*? Just what kind of bird are you? Come, let's meet more Unique Birds. . . .

Did you ever
skip along the Milky Way
and pick a bouquet of moonbeans?
No? Well, the next U B
can show you the way. . . . .

PONDER
The Dreamer

36

ℙONDER

ambles through life in low gear

With back to the world and a far-away look in the eyes, this can be none other than Ponder. Sensitive, dreaming dreams, peeking only now and then at reality. This bird's approach to life is indicated in the words on a wooden plaque that Ponder cherishes—"Why worry? Today is the tomorrow you were worried about yesterday."

Indeed, to Ponder, life is not a challenge but a pathway along which to experience love, joy, harmony. Ponder finds beauty everywhere, in simple everyday sights and sounds—the rhapsody of crickets on a summer night, a playful kitten chasing a prankish leaf, the glorious sky at sunrise and sunset.

But the work-a-day world is another matter. Its whizzing whirl is distasteful, almost painful, to Ponder. Of all birds, Ponder is probably the least competitive, which causes some to call this U B lazy, lacking ambition. Possibly there is a smidgen of laziness, but the greater truth is that Ponder's internal drive is simply set in low gear. From Ponder's view, the real world clinks and clanks like a huge machine in need of repair. The billowy white clouds of fantasy provide a very essential escape hatch.

Some dreamers go on for years escaping reality, barely keeping body and soul together. They have deep emotions that tend to confuse them. They seem more aware of their limitations than their talents. You can help. Give the dreamer you know some encouragement, direction, and perhaps a push to channel the mental and emotional meanderings into creative endeavors—music, art, photography, or designing, writing—anything to utilize those artistic abilities which may be latent, but are there; if not as a career, then as a hobby.

Ponder is one of the fortunate dreamers who broke the shell of inner doubt and timidity, who resisted taking the "easy path," and gradually carved out a successful career in the creative arts. Somewhat in awe, Ponder says, "I'm making more money than I ever dreamed possible, and I'm very grateful. But it is the inner satisfaction that means the most to me. When I am quietly creating, I feel in tune with the universe. My heart sings! If only I could help others feel the same joy!"

This deep concern for other U Bs is the reason, no doubt, that Ponder has a ready, sympathetic ear for anyone in trouble. Ponder can listen to family problems, personal resentments, job injustices, love tangles—the worst of woes—without shock or critical judgment, and then give all possible aid. There is, of course, a wonderful by-product. All those riled-up emotions of others provide valuable input for Ponder's internal "computer," to be called forth later in creative works.

Despite all those BITs of compassion and misty dreaminess, Ponder has spurts of live-wire outgoingness. Ponder has a perky sense of humor, not in telling jokes but making quips in reaction to a situation or remark. Clever of mind, Ponder can be caustic or comical, whimsical or witty, delivering hilarious one-liners with a face of stone.

A non-conformer, Ponder finds it difficult to become routine with anything. You are meeting for lunch? Do not expect Ponder to be on time. But be ready to hear an imaginative, possibly wild and crazy, excuse. Just remember, that is part of the charm of this U B. Ponder's sentimental nature, kindness and warm friendliness are other qualities that make this bird delightful to know.

But, of course, Ponder has some negative BITs. Doesn't every U B? Ponder can provide exasperating moments for family and friends for shortcomings in practical, everyday matters—"I thought *you* were getting the groceries." For extravagance—"I couldn't resist buying it." For vagueness—"Did I say I'd call?" In response, if you flare up, be aware that your harshness can hurt this sensitive bird to the quick. But Ponder would never reveal it. The reaction would be a wisecrack, indifference or sharp sarcasm; whatever it is, it's a camouflage for true feelings, possibly of vulnerability or a sense of privacy. Or is it a little game of deception, a product of that fertile imagination?

Take care that you do not criticize Ponder time after time. That could trigger a siege of despondency. You are dealing with a gentle, humble spirit, one that needs supportive love and reassurance.

We could never survive this clanging, banging planet without the Ponders. They bring the wonderfully soothing magic of make-believe to all of us. How could we face reality, day after day, if we didn't occasionally float on a cloud and catch a star! More moonbeams, Ponder, more!

Can you picture yourself as Ponder—the creative, compassionate dreamer?

A summary of Ponder's BITs:
Views life through rose-colored glasses; humble, sentimental, sensitive; helpful and kind; creative; perky sense of humor; broadminded; noncompetitive; does not excite easily; lacks discipline, ambition; daydreams; impractical, vague, careless; easily discouraged; a sympathetic listener; deep concern for others; loves and appreciates beauty.

Don't blink.
If you do, you could miss
that clever, quick-as-lightning,
competitive U B. . . . .

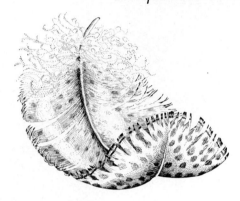

JETT
The Doer

JETT

tackles everything with feverish energy

How typical of Jett to zoom in and out! The moment one job is finished, it is rush, rush to another.

A supercharged doer, Jett never undertakes a task. Jett attacks it. When this U B is in action, the very atmosphere vibrates with energy. Huge workloads disappear so fast you wonder, could there be two of Jett?

Doing several things at once comes naturally to Jett and seems to fulfill an inner need. Believe it or not, this "tiger" of a bird can carry on a couple of busy telephone conversations (Jett has four phones), give orders to others at hand, greet visitors and look over a stack of mail, seemingly all at the same time, like a well-oiled, multi-armed, two-headed whirling dervish. To Jett this is merely routine.

What if the task is tough, the situation impossible? Does this throw Jett into a tailspin? Never. This U B throbs with resourcefulness and raring-to-go diligence. With eyes ablaze, Jett digs and digs until the solution is found, even if it means working around the clock to meet a deadline.

This reveals a special BIT in Jett—pride in excelling. That is true not only at work but at play. On the tennis court, for exam-ple, Jett is fiercely competitive. Everyone likes to win, but with Jett there seems to be an inner force, like a powerful revved up motor, impelling Jett to win.

Is Jett more machine than mortal? Positively not. Jett is tenderhearted and sympathetic, belying an inborn coolness of nature. If you need help with a perplexing problem, you can count on Jett to come up with clever angles and a pep talk. Jett knows that, even at the darkest hour, you can carry on when new hope is set aflame in one's breast. But beware! When you ask for help, do not snare this U B into a series of tedious, mundane duties. If you do, you will see the pleasant disposition dissolve, wham-bam, into a rude, blunt bundle of irritability. Jett is impatient and detests monotony. Jett's spirit must soar!

Jett likes people... loves to communicate. Want a sparkler at your next party? Invite Jett. Your guests will be enthralled with this vibrant, scintillating bird.

But do not expect Jett to be a listener. Not that Jett is an egotist who demands "center stage." Definitely not. Jett simply has an insatiable desire to communicate ideas and information. Jett speaks with great logic and is armed with up-to-date facts.

Another tip: Jett is un—yes, UNpredictable. Just because Jett was the Big, Sexy Charmer yesterday does not mean that the same glow will radiate today. Other things now occupy this dynamo's mind. So Jett might act aloof, be sarcastic to your soupçon of conversation, or even rudely belittle you. You may wonder, "What did I do?" Nothing at all! Forget the rebuff because Jett will. In fact, if confronted with it later, Jett is likely to reply, "I never said that!" or "You didn't hear right." Just remember, it is this U B's nature to be changeable and very direct.

But do not misunderstand. Jett can be a delightful pal when the spirit dictates. Lively and fun, ready for some new adventure. Jett loves activity, new vistas, new projects.

There may be times you feel you do not know Jett at all. Is it the unpredictableness, the innate coolness? Or is it because Jett is hiding true feelings, or possibly disguising true intent? There is a BIT of cunning in Jett.

And have you noticed the restlessness? Is it the need for variety and change, the inquisitive nature, or simply that Jett is never satisfied to rest on yesterday's accomplishments? Ever on the wing, Jett seems always to be seeking betterment. In fact, friends declare that somehow, some way, this U B WILL better the entire world. All that drive! All those ideas, and ideals!

Thank goodness for the Jetts in our midst. They get things done, on the double. Without a doubt, they will blaze a trail right into the twenty first century, giving new aspirations and new hope to us all. Blaze on, ye Jetts, blaze on!!

Do you have the specialness of Jett—the ingenious, dynamic doer?

A summary of Jett's BITs:
Quick-acting, intense, supercharged; impatient, inconsistent and unpredictable; tenderhearted; ingenious, clever and versatile; logical, inquiring mind; likes variety and change; blunt, flippant, aloof; cunning, rude and direct; innately cool nature; belittles others; loves to communicate; strives to excel; stays up-to-date.

Give a big hug
to the next Unique Bird.
You'll see why. . . . .

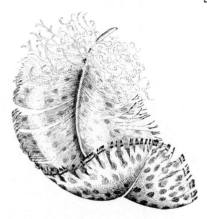

STEDDY
The Solid Citizen

STEDDY

admit to stubbornness? Never!

This crazy, mixed-up world could use more U Bs like Steddy! Honest and dependable. Hard-working. Easy-going. Even disposition, patient. Sensible, solid, steady. Serene. But stubborn. Yes, stubborn, stubborn, STUBBORN!

Does the sun rise in the East? Does day follow night? You have as much chance of changing Steddy's mind as changing the laws of nature.

If you are wise, you will not pick at or cross this mountain of fixed matter. Steddy is slow to "blow," thanks to an immense reservoir of patience, but when it is drained dry, look out. The sleeping volcano erupts. Better that you let the mountain be with nary a word about obstinacy. Did you ever meet a stubborn U B who would admit to being mulish? Of course not. They are patient, persevering or persistent; sensible or standing firm.

No doubt about it, Steddy does have these and other exemplary BITs—strength of character, warmth of personality, and a placid presence that seems to bring a soothing restfulness to the very atmosphere. However, there are times that placid presence tends to resemble lethargy. Steddy simply cannot jump into action and do any unplanned task *now*. "I can't change my plans," protests Steddy even while appearing unbusy. This bird is just not a fast mover. This bird cannot be pushed.

If you are highly energetic yourself, you may look upon Steddy as a procrastinator or even a lazy bird, but remember, it is Steddy's style to plan carefully and proceed with caution. Any job promised will get done eventually. If you happen to be on the waiting end and your patience runs low, try a little "handling"—cheerful suggestions, some praise, a helping hand. With a big smile, you might suggest, "Come on, let's tackle this together. You're a pro, show me how to help." Steddy finds it hard to resist bubbling togetherness and affection. A word of caution: do not "maneuver" when Steddy is worn out. You will not succeed, and you will have a grouch on your hands. Steddy needs more rest than most birds.

Under emotional stress or during adversity, Steddy is very stoic. Never complains or nags. Never seeks sympathy or broods. Steddy quietly exercises great self-control.

But do not think those powers of endurance and emotional stability make Steddy an insensitive creature. This U B has senses keen as a tuning fork. Hear the siren in the distance? Of course not, but Rover does. And so does Steddy.

These acute senses reveal an artistic bird. Steddy loves music and the other arts, but for diversion, not as a career. And, unlike artists who can suffer poverty for their art, Steddy loves a feeling of wealth. Steddy takes pride in possessions, in buying quality, yet always has a sharp eye for bargains. But nothing frivolous. That's wasteful.

What is the basis for Steddy's desire for wealth and material comforts? "Materialism," chortle unperceptive birds. Actually, Steddy must fulfill a deep-seated need for security. This BIT causes Steddy to strive industriously to get ahead, to accumulate wealth and to avoid risks of any type. "Why take chances on what you have?" Blessed with good business sense, Steddy willingly accepts greater and greater responsibility, but not for power. It is for security.

This firm BIT of playing it safe causes Steddy to be very protective of both loved ones and possessions. You need to borrow a car? Don't ask Steddy. "I can't lend you my car, but I'll drive you." Basically, this U B has a generous heart.

Some birds find Steddy too slow-moving, too bland, much too locked into routine and—well, frankly—boring. All that steadfastness and calmness come off dull and drab to those U Bs who thrive on fire and ice. But Steddy's attitude is "I am who I am." Steddy has no desire to be a razzle-dazzle bird, or any other type. Steddy just happens to be comfortable with Steddy's own self. A positive BIT, indeed, to feel self-esteem.

Steddy firmly believes and often advises—"Be yourself, bird, and respect yourself for all your good qualities. That's where respect for others begins—with yourself." Wise counsel from good ol' Steddy.

How fortunate for all of us U Bs to have these ever reliable, solid citizens among us! The Steddys of the world are the ballast that keeps our earthly ship on course. Give the Steddy you know a big hug! To show your appreciation!

Are there similarities between you and Steddy—the patient, reliable, solid citizen?

A summary of Steddy's BITs:
Easy-going, calm, even disposition; patient and reliable; warm nature; stubborn; slow-moving, cautious; procrastinates; resists change; locked into routine; sensible, steady and solid; hard-working and persistent; angers when crossed; self-indulgent; possessive; needs to feel secure; practical; good sense of values.

No doubt about it,
the next Unique Bird
entrances almost everyone. . . . . .

PLUME

exudes charm without even trying

Soak up the sunshine of this delightfully personable U B! Plume radiates the joy and wonder of living. Even the plumage—its magnificence inspired Plume's name—bespeaks this bird's charm.

Who could *not* be attracted by the colorful feathers, the expressive eyes, the restrained sensuality? Plume can enter a roomful of U Bs and moments later be surrounded, especially by those of the opposite sex. Plume just smiles and talks, and in the most effortless, ingratiating way completely captivates everyone. It is pure, unadulterated charisma. It emanates like rays from the sun.

There are times Plume "performs"—when the mood, the audience, or the setting is right. Plume can act out a story, mimic others, tell a crazy joke and thoroughly enjoy the momentary limelight of ham acting; yet, in private, Plume will confess to BITs of shyness. "I struggle to overcome it by making myself step forward and speak up. But that inner tendency to hang back always haunts me."

Sensitive, modest and gentle, Plume is also neat, methodical, practical; discriminating and fastidious. And FINICKY. Without a doubt, Plume qualifies as the world's Number One perfectionist. Take Plume's personal habits. Plume does not just get dressed. Plume gets meticulously groomed. Look at Plume's files, any of them. They are kept precisely and completely. The lawn—Plume does not mow it. Plume manicures it! What about food? Here perfection is ever elusive. The toast is too light or too dark; the boiled egg is too soft or too hard. No one can be fussier than Plume.

And Heaven to Betsy, do NOT use four-letter words in Plume's presence. Not because of prudishness. It is because Plume abhors vulgarity. The same applies to sloppiness. This BIT, a penchant for neatness and orderliness, unveils the other side of Plume's personality.

Plume can pick, pick, pick if shoes are left lying around the house, if tools are not put back on the well-organized rack, if papers are strewn about the living room, or anything else left out of place. Or if you fail to be on time. Plume knows the meaning of punctuality, and if you are in any part of Plume's life, you soon do too.

Another "no, no" with Plume is any display of stupidity. If you happen to be the culprit who created a mess with a hasty decision, for example, or perhaps mindlessly insulted someone, be ready for a verbal whipping and lecture on how to improve. But do not let it upset you or gnaw at you later. Just know that it is a fixed BIT in Plume to criticize and correct. Plume really does mean to be of help, without any intention of disparaging you. And Plume's advice usually proves worthwhile!

PLUME
The Charmer

49

$\mathcal{P}$LUME

If ever you do lose your "cool" and counterattack Plume's negative BITs, you soon discover that Plume is not equipped to "take it." Already well aware of shortcomings, Plume wishes no reminders, thank you. Your onslaught can provoke crankiness or a siege of sulkiness. Remember, this U B is supersensitive. A quiet suggestion to Plume is as effective as a shouted command to other types of birds.

But back to the charm. What makes Plume GLOW? Perhaps it is the aura of "something wonderful is happening in my life"—the free-flowing, joyful spirit that ever encompasses Plume. Or a consciousness of NOW, that today is the day to LIVE. Plume avows that "tomorrow is forever out of your grasp so it is this day, this hour, this moment from which you pour your cup of joy."

Or could Plume's "love affair" with love be the wellspring of all that charm? To Plume, love DOES make the world go round. Love *who* you are and *what* you are, or love becoming what you want to be. Love your family and friends, your home and community. Love your work and your play, and most important of all, love God. "God is my Partner," declares Plume, "my closest companion."

Plume's approach to living is special, indeed, and surely a blessing from Heaven Above. In an almost childlike way, Plume appears aware of this blessing.

You, too, are blessed if you have a Plume in your circle. Somehow, grey skies turn blue and life becomes a beautiful adventure when Plume is about. Love and kisses to all of you wonderfully charming Plumes!

Do your traits match those of Plume—the modest, meticulous charmer?

A summary of Plume's BITs:
Joyful spirit; warm, charming personality; modest and gentle; meticulous; a perfectionist; finicky; hypercritical; corrects others; fussy and hard to please; frets easily; sulks when criticized; hates to admit when wrong; sensitive; discriminating and fastidious; abhors vulgarity; dislikes stupidity, carelessness; softhearted, loving and romantic; loves neatness and orderliness; talent for detail.

It was bound to happen!
When you have a friendly fireball
and a gregarious optimist in the
same group, a discussion begins. . . . . .

Understanding others better

Flash

Breez

Woe

FLASH: Now, let me make my point. Most of the birds I know have problems, and they're always blaming others. Well, we should look to ourselves. That's where the fault lies. We expect the worst instead of the best. We hug our fears, our hurts, our hatreds. No wonder things go wrong! Why, sometimes I feel as though the whole world is sinking in a sea of negative BITs.

BREEZ: Relax, Flash, relax. Don't be a gloom-glubber. Life is a game, not a death sentence. Be happy! Enjoy!

PRANCE: You're right, Breez. Life IS a game, and you yourself are the *most important* player. You agree, don't you, Ponder?

PONDER: Ah . . . well . . . I don't know. I'll have to think about it. I'll go into the woods where it's quiet. Want to come along, Steddy?

STEDDY: I can't come now, Ponder. I have my day planned. Maybe tomorrow.

WOE: Nobody asked me what I think. You always ignore me.

PLUME: Now, Woe, don't always feel left out. You shouldn't take that attitude. You have to speak up and simply voice your opinion. Now, I think life is very much like a game. What do you think, Jett?

JETT: Don't bother me, Plume, with all this nonsense about life being a game. My games are chess and tennis. Now, leave me alone. I'm busy on a big project.

SAGE: Of course. Jett is always busy getting things done. You know, we all reveal our own unique nature by what we say and do. Breez's comment shows a fun-loving spirit. Woe feels neglected. Ponder is slow-moving, and Steddy has to make plans before doing anything.

FLASH: How about getting back to negative BITs?

SAGE: Okay, persistent bird! Well, we all know that we are

born with negative personality traits as well as positive. But what appears negative to one may seem positive to another. Our own individual traits determine *how we perceive* and *how we react* to the BITs of others.

Take our own Flash, as an example. Flash's excitability causes Flash to be labeled a fireball. Breez, as an outgoing, happy-go-lucky being, reacts positively to Flash and sees Flash as a lively, interesting bird. So does Prance. The big ego in Prance precludes any sense of domination by Flash. But Woe is a bird of another feather. Woe, being very sensitive and insecure, looks upon Flash as pushy and loud.

Prance

FLASH: Pushy and *loud*???

SAGE: Not to me, Flash. I see you as a vibrant, enjoyable bird. But please let me finish my thought. A trait that seems objectionable to one bird may be readily acceptable to another. We all see each other differently. But that does not make either of us right or wrong, or good or bad. We are just different.

BREEZ: That's what's fun—knowing birds different from yourself. They give you new outlooks, keep life exciting.

Jett

FLASH: Especially if they throw a jealous fit like I do sometimes. But nobody enjoys that irritating trait.

SAGE: No one likes jealous outbursts, to be sure. They cause certain types of birds to retaliate in anger or other negative emotions. But a tolerant, compassionate type would respond with understanding. This bird would try to rise above the frailty and help the jealous bird.

JETT: Bean Sprouts! Some birds don't understand anything but a firm voice and assertive action. Give them an inch, they'll take a mile.

PRANCE: I agree. Keep them in line, that's my advice.

Ponder

Plume

Steddy

PONDER: I'm sure that's good advice for certain types of birds, but I think the main point here is not *how* we should react to each other. The main point is that, because we are different, we *do* react differently to each other. And we shouldn't try to force *our* way on somebody else, nor expect others to react like us.

STEDDY: I try to be understanding of birds that aren't my type, even when they give me a hard time. You never know what stresses that bird might be enduring, or what "hurts" that bird might be carrying inside.

PRANCE: Your halo is GLORIOUS, Steddy!

SAGE: Yes, Steddy is a very tolerant being. Also, perhaps we should remind ourselves that "difficult" birds just might be "yelling" at themselves when they attack others. All of us occasionally show irritations to others when, unconsciously of course, we are really rebelling at some problem or hurt in our own lives. And, of course, we all know that we should make an effort to keep our own negative emotions under control. The more we are aware of them and control them, the easier it is to deal positively with, and not be distressed by, the negative qualities in others.

PRANCE: So don't get stuck in the mud of your own "uglies"!

SAGE: Right! And, as Breez said earlier, look at life as a game. Keep your sense of humor. Enjoy!

Let's meet the next U B. . . . .

*Ready or not,
here comes
your leader. . . . . .*

BOOM

gives the orders. Now march!

Listen! Is that Boom? Of course. Nobody else sounds quite like THAT! It is Boom taking charge, telling everybody what to do, whether they already know or not.

Boom loves to give orders, to show importance. But it is not conceit or a desire to be the center of attention that motivates Boom to be bossy. Repeat, bossy! It is a giant size BIT—an inborn sense of leadership, plus a sizable dash of selfishness in wanting things done "my way." And RIGHT NOW! Boom expects others to follow, simply without question. "I need helpers, not managers or complainers."

In groups Boom performs as a leader with a natural no-nonsense authority, but in close personal relationships Boom assumes an almost childlike naivete in playing the boss. "I know how to do it." The wise mate knows that this U B needs to be in charge. That brings out the best. So does recognition of Boom's considerable talents. However, compliments must be sincere; Boom holds contempt for gushy flattery. The same holds true for slave-like obedience. Leaders like to live and work with equals.

Is there a Boom somewhere in your life? Do you find yourself on the receiving end of authoritative commands? You usually go along with the game, but there are times you suddenly, surprisingly, lash out. That is verboten, right? The bossy U B becomes enraged. Nobody tells Boom where to go and what to do!! You are pelted with a torrential rain of vexatious verbiage. Wow! This bird does nothing halfway or with subtle diplomacy. Open and direct, that's Boom, even if it means thoughtless disregard for the feelings of others.

Thankfully, Boom's temper fades as quickly as it flares. And Boom never really means all those cutting remarks. This explosive bird forgets fast and assumes you do too; this bird never holds grudges and can apologize when need be. But, it is wise to remember, Boom must be boss. Leaders never follow.

As you might expect of an impulsive, independent bird, Boom has strong likes and dislikes, and brashly tries to force these set opinions on others. It just does not occur to this U B to "sell you" instead of tell you.

But Boom is not all blunt bossiness and "my way" self-centeredness. Far from it! The same strength and fire that underlie Boom's dominating nature also make Boom a devoted and generous friend. Warmhearted and cheerful. Boom jumps quickly to do favors for others, in full-cup-running-over measure. Boom sees the need through to the end, long after others have tippy-toed out of the picture. A commendable BIT, indeed.

If you happen to be a recipient of help from Boom, watch how this U B reacts to

BOOM
The Big Boss

your words of gratitude. Just laps them up! All birds need praise and recognition, but with Boom there seems to be a real thirst for approval and appreciation. It is part of Boom's need to be liked and admired. Of course, the Big Chief would never admit it.

What do you do when you want to criticize this headstrong, feisty bird? Well, you had better be clever about it! Criticism falls on deaf ears or prompts an outburst. So turn your negative words into a compliment or a request. Do not complain, "You're doing a terrible job." Rephrase it, such as, "That task calls for a genius. I wonder, is it possible to do it this way?" Then make your suggestion. Those words are more likely to be heard. Remember, Boom likes doing something for others and, of course, knows a lot more about it (or thinks so) than you do.

Boom *loves* new ventures, is a crusader at heart. Almost all birds might take a cue from Boom, who likes to advise: "Reach out for new interests. Sitting still or drifting invites stagnation, boredom. Undertake a challenge, a new project, big or small. That's how you stay ALIVE!"

Big and tough challenges are the kind Boom likes, thanks to a generous supply of positive BITs—an adventurous spirit, tremendous drive, an enterprising nature; inventiveness and cleverness when necessary. But no trickery. No devious ways. Boom has a straightforwardness that is laudable, plus boundless enthusiasm. Boom joyfully bounces from one wave of enthusiasm to another. All qualities of a leader? You know it!

Where, oh where, would civilization be without these visionary, pioneering, forceful U Bs? Maybe still in the Dark Ages. A low bow to these leaders!

Do you resemble Boom—the impulsive, independent, big boss?

A summary of Boom's BITs:
Great drive; likes to take charge; feels important; bossy; open and direct; adventurous spirit; courageous and enterprising; selfish; "my way, me first" self-centeredness; wants everything NOW; fixed opinions; independent and impulsive; quick-tempered; needs to be admired; generous, optimistic, enthusiastic; forceful leader.

The droopsies got you
dragging your tail?
A sure cure
is a visit with Ripple. . . . .

RIPPLE

relates "funnies" at the perfect moment

No one will dispute it, Ripple loves to talk. Lots of birds do! But, of course, there are many types of talkers. There is the buzzing busybody, a self-appointed "private eye and ear," ready to report to anybody who will listen. That is NOT Ripple.

Then there is the chattering chickadee who twitters endlessly on trivia. That is NOT Ripple. Nor is the blowhard bulging with self, nor the authority with all the answers. Not the fanatic with a cause, or the bore with an ocean of details. Is Ripple a fast-talking salesman? Politician? No. No.

So, who *is* Ripple??? Okay, Ripple is a lighthearted, bubbling storyteller. Not of jokes, but witty descriptions of recent experiences or happenings. Ripple sees color and humor in almost everything. The world is a big, exciting passing parade. This lovable, charming U B can transform even a ho-hum incident into a glory story—bigger and brighter than life, but what fun! Little nothings sizzle and pop when Ripple tells them.

You probably have a Ripple in your life. A contented, cheerful bird. Agreeable, gracious, always making you feel at ease. Except—isn't there always an exception!—when Ripple is betwixt and between about something.

Nobody can seesaw back and forth more than Ripple when faced with making a decision. "I've changed my mind. Do you think I'm making a mistake?...If only I knew what's ahead...Maybe I shouldn't change my mind." You can review the alternatives. You can suggest. You can push. But Ripple will not be rushed. Yes, a BIT of obstinacy takes hold. Better that you just be patient and try to be helpful; realize that Ripple turns to you as a trusted friend and really values your advice. Give it carefully! Ripple is influenced very easily by others. In fact, Ripple has a reputation for being gullible. The first to admit it, Ripple laughingly says, "I was born wide-eyed and innocent, and I guess I'll die that way."

However, do not label this bird a lame-brain because of that gullibility (or is it faith in human nature?) and that irksome BIT of "should I or shouldn't I." Ripple is blessed with an intelligent, sharp mind and just happens to have an inner need to weigh and judge every angle before making a decision. A strong sense of fairness and justice further compels this U B to approach decisions with a truckload of options.

But that built-in teeter-totter is far outweighed by many positive BITs. Ripple lives by lofty principles, generously helps others, is a natural peacemaker. Few can match Ripple's finesse at smoothing ruffled feathers, on one bird or a whole flock. Ripple hates discord. When tempers begin to flare, Ripple speaks up and with great skill points out all the positives, cleverly mini-

RIPPLE
The Talker

mizing all the negatives and springing little "funnies" to make everyone laugh—and start cooing again. A born diplomat!

Like many birds, Ripple has contradictions in certain qualities. For example, Ripple loves harmony but can turn suddenly cranky or sulky. Ripple excels at peacemaking but can become argumentative, sometimes seemingly just for the sake of argument. Ripple can hold center stage, relating story after story, then become a wonderful listener. Ripple detests crowds, yet has a dread of loneliness so seeks friendship or partnership. Ripple can appear lazy by taking eons to get started on "whatever," probably due to some indecision, and then work furiously for hours or days on end. But, is there any rule that insists Ripple must be consistent?

If you happen to need a friend on a "blue Monday," Ripple can be your haven.

Almost like magic, Ripple's wholesomeness, winsomeness and glow of aliveness transform your droopsies into jollies. You don't want to hop a space ship to the moon after all!

The longer you know Ripple the more you realize that Ripple's talk is mostly "happy talk." Not by accident, but by design. Ripple knows that happiness does not fall from Heaven, blessing some and not others. You must seek it. Happiness comes as a reward for work well done, leisure time well spent, for overcoming weaknesses, for "doing" for others and especially for love shared. Every day Ripple seems to create happiness, for others and in turn for self.

My, how bleak our lives would be without the Ripples in our midst! They are a fountain of joy and harmony. They are peacemakers. Please, Divine Power, send flocks of Ripples everywhere. Now!

Are you "cut from the same cloth" as Ripple—the diplomatic, happy talker?

A summary of Ripple's BITs:
Likes to express self; diplomatic and agreeable; gracious, refined; cheerful and contented; talkative; good sense of humor; indecisive; gullible and naive; changes mind; at times argumentative; tends to exaggerate; dreads loneliness; fair-minded; strong sense of justice; charming ways; loves harmony; a natural peacemaker.

*If you're in competition
with the next U B,
good luck!
You just may need it. . . . .*

EMBER
The Achiever

EMBER

ever undaunted, strides steadily to that goal

Where is Ember headed with that determined, "going somewhere" walk? Right up the ladder of success! But inconspicuously.

You are fortunate to catch a glimpse of Ember striding with that great sense of purpose. Usually this shy, unassuming bird does not appear to be going anywhere, especially UP. Well, that placid exterior reveals nothing of what's inside—a brightly burning ember, aglow with determination and drive. Important BITs for getting ahead.

Every day in every way Ember moves calmly, assuredly and directly toward Ember's goals. Whatever they are, they involve authority and position; they command respect and provide security. But there is no frantic scurrying, no pushing of self before others. This U B has a low-key, get-things-done demeanor, an easy, steady confidence. Everything is carefully planned and efficiently executed, including the daily chores of living.

Sound like a rigid, no-fun way of life? To carefree, less motivated birds, definitely "yes." But to Ember, the smooth-running, disciplined mode of living is a necessity. "Goofing off" is for playbirds or lazy loons. Time is valuable! Goals must be attained!

Ember loves—dearly loves—to work, to achieve. Not just for the dollar, though that is important because Ember does like the material comforts it can bring; it is more for the intangible rewards of accomplishment—the pride, the fulfillment, the esteem of others. Ember may pretend to be unconcerned about compliments or admiration of others and may even react with embarrassment, but like most birds, needs respect and praise. And, isn't accomplishment hollow unless you can share your joy with others?

Some birds call Ember a workaholic. That is mostly true, but not to the extent that family members are neglected. Ember feels a deep sense of duty and devotion to family, even to the point of self-sacrifice. If someone must do without, Ember quietly "makes do." No complaints. No martyrdom. Just an abiding sense of responsibility. But Ember is not without personal emotional needs. Despite all that ambition and self-sufficiency, Ember has a soft heart that calls for love and closeness. If you happen to belong to Ember's family, tell Ember you appreciate, you care.

However, do not be fooled by this bird's gentle side. It has a starched backing. Ember can be strict and stern when others shirk their duties, disregard directions, lack good ethics or otherwise fail to meet high standards. The cool, firm hand of discipline stems from abundant BITs of seriousness. Ember simply was born with a practical, sensible, over-exacting bent of mind ... plus an almost burdensome conscientiousness.

EMBER

Would you call Ember a "stick in the mud?" At times, probably yes; certainly not a bouncy, happy-go-lucky bird—a type, by the way, that Ember secretly yearns to be. Well aware of those introvertish, nose-to-the-grindstone BITs, Ember strives to be less duty-bound, even a little frivolous. But the deep vein of steadiness, that solid core of self-discipline, make it anything but easy. Of course, a difficult task does not phase Ember. If it is easy, where is the fun? Where is the sense of accomplishment?

If you have an Ember flying in your flock, you most likely have noted the great respect this U B has for others—young, old, rich or poor. Obviously, this also means respect for self, a valuable virtue in climbing that ladder. Like many purposeful birds, Ember is very courteous and has natural good manners.

Ember has a good sense of humor, smiles and laughs easily. But that pleasant disposition can become broody if subjected to repeated teasing or criticism, or kidding about something important. To this U B, life is serious!

Ember shies away from mob-scene parties unless they can be useful for career or social stature. Then they will be endured, but that inner timidity is ever present. However, Ember delights in conversations one-to-one or with a few friends. For entertainment, Ember loves the theater or a concert. This ambitious U B definitely has a creative side that calls for nourishment. But the greatest joy still comes while at work!

Well, the world needs determined, goal-oriented achievers. All humanity needs more disciplined, more self-respecting beings. Thank you, all you Embers! Your quiet diligence and your accomplishments benefit us all.

Are you "the spittin' image" of Ember—the shy, disciplined achiever?

A summary of Ember's BITs:
Ambitious, determined, goal-oriented; shy and unassuming; well-mannered; unduly duty-bound and conscientious; self-sacrificing; over-serious and over-exacting; responsible, self-disciplined; low-key, easy confidence; poor mixer socially; broods when criticized; strict and stern; needs respect; practical, tenacious, thorough; devoted to family.

Do you sometimes think
YOU are a little crazy?
Well, match your wackiness
with that of the next U B. . . . .

YAZOO

springs surprises as easily as birds fly

Is this bird a little kooky... has the world gone ga-ga... or is it you who has one foot stuck in a rut? Who knows! Right now, meet Yazoo—pure delight, playing the clown.

High-spirited and frolicsome at the moment, Yazoo also can be a tease. In fun, not in torment. And Yazoo can be a great humanitarian filled with brotherly love, or a sympathetic friend, even a detective if you happen to have a mystery or puzzle disturbing you. Thanks to intense curiosity, Yazoo loves to probe and analyze. And what intuition! Yazoo comes up with ideas that never occur to less gifted minds.

But suddenly, without warning, that attentive, sincere friend can rebuff you and become downright distant. Why? Well, it is probably a matter of priorities in Yazoo's mind. Devotion to a cause could be the reason. Yazoo is almost always knee-deep in some project to serve mankind or to preserve Mother Nature. If you fail to share Yazoo's enthusiasm, the humanitarian cause wins; your friendship is placed on "hold."

Once you understand this unbending BIT in Yazoo's makeup, you no longer feel rejected. Also, once you realize that Yazoo's ardent interest in you is a "sometime" thing, you get over the uneasiness that you have offended in some way. This U B simply does not conform to the usual habits of friendship, or anything else. But that does not cause Yazoo to suffer a lack of friends: There are dozens, up and down the social ladder. Many of them refer to Yazoo as the rebel. The more staid ones say "eccentric."

Yazoo takes pride in the rebel label, and it does free Yazoo to be as different, as independent, original, and "way out" as the spirit dictates. "Who cares what other birds think!" declares Yazoo. If there is disapproval, "I just look the other way." No doubt, this is one of the reasons Yazoo has scores of casual friendships but few really close ones. Yazoo seems to prefer to remain a little detached, perhaps because there are times being alone is best—to dream a few dreams, to commune with one's inner being.

The cool, unemotional nature of Yazoo makes this U B pretty difficult to catch in marriage. Many a bird of this type has stretched friendship for years before agreeing to coo "I do." Once caught, no bird is more loyal or faithful.

Of course, the partner must be very understanding of the rebel's lack of sentiment and the need to feel free and independent. But isn't that part of marriage? To accept one another as you are, and to adjust to each other's needs, strengths and shortcomings. With love and understanding. And with a ready sense of humor.

Take Yazoo's absentmindedness, for ex-

YAZOO
The Rebel

ample. Nothing is going to change this BIT, so you might as well laugh and have fun over the "fallout" from it. And Yazoo's bag of surprises! You might as well enjoy an impromptu picnic breakfast to watch the sunrise or the silly signs Yazoo stuck on the bathroom ceiling. Or how about this—Yazoo greeting party guests from the roof. Hold on, there is more! In top hat and tails —whoop-dee-do antics that burst into Yazoo's head like exploding rockets.

One thing is certain—life around Yazoo is seldom dull, except perhaps when Yazoo is played out or lost in solitude. That is dull? No, it is a welcome respite, a chance to recharge. For everybody!

Friend or relative, you would never dream of curbing Yazoo's sometimes bizarre capers or unconventional ideas. You agree with Yazoo that you should be tolerant of idiosyncrasies in others. "We all have our quirks," says Yazoo. "I'll overlook yours if you'll overlook mine."

Is this cheerful, forgetful, unpredictable, independent U B a bird-brain? Assuredly not! Yazoo is smart, with flashes of brilliance. Yazoo is conscientious, perceptive and progressive. However, making money is not a driving force in Yazoo. Making friends is more important, and being free to do all those offbeat things.

If it were not for the rebels flying among us, all creation might be stuck in a rut. We need inventiveness, novel ideas and idealism, plus a little impracticality to carry us forward into the future. And we need some surprises to shake the sleep from our eyes. More Yazoos! More! More!

Are you "one of a kind" like Yazoo—the inventive, absentminded rebel?

A summary of Yazoo's BITs:
Original, curious, analytical; inventive and independent; rebellious; unemotional, cool nature; unconventional; friendly and loyal; high-spirited; conscientious; absentminded; unpredictable; perverse, possibly eccentric; perceptive and progressive; a free thinker; idealistic; a reformer, humanitarian, and a tease.

Now, the time has come . . . . .

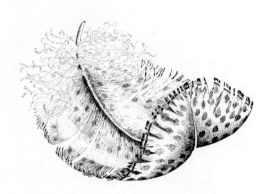

GOOD-BYE...

Yes, the time has come to say good-bye. We must fly our separate ways.

Thank you for the time we have spent together. Thank you for being you, special you.

Before we part, I want to hear you say it, with feeling—"I am special!"

Terrific!

Now, don't you forget it!

Birds are special too

How drab our world would be without birds! Their lilting songs, colorful plumage, their lively movements are a delight to behold.

Are you a bird watcher, casual or serious? Then, you must have observed that birds, like us, have personalities. Among the many types are leaders, quiet thinkers, expressive extroverts.

The latter brings blue jays to mind. They appear at times to be rather raucous showoffs, perhaps even bullies, but that is only a guise. Blue jays are the protectors or policemen of the bird world. When an enemy approaches in the form of a cat or dog, blue jays shriek a call of danger to all. Watch. It's fun to see. Blue jays are also magnanimous, allowing smaller birds to eat as they stand guard. True, the blue jays at this bird lover's home know that food is plentiful. But their protective nature is still worth noting.

So are the calls and songs of birds. They all seem to carry a message. Do you imagine it too? When you happen to awaken very early as dawn is breaking, those subdued, tentative chirps seem to be whispering, "I'm awake . . . are you?" During the day, their enthusiastic bursts of song seem to shout to the world, "Sing, sing! Be happy!" At eventide their songs become a dialog. They call and answer each other as though to say, "Come, let's rest." . . . "No, not yet." . . . "Yes, the day is done." Gradually, the dialog ends. The birds sleep.

To this writer, birds are the joyful spirit of the universe, Nature's gift to humankind. They are, indeed, very special!

*I*ndex

With a check list of each bird's BITs

What Kind of Bird Are You? Just for fun, you may want to sort out *your* traits on the check list below. If you do, check the BITs that best describe you. You'll soon see the bird or birds that are YOU.

Please note that BITs attributed to each bird are not necessarily exclusive to that bird, nor appear in the same combination or degree in other birds. And if some birds seem to have contradictory characteristics, remember that many beings are born with a dual nature.

BIRDS and their predominant BITs (Built-In Traits):

Page

BREEZ — the frank, outgoing optimist. 15–18

— very optimistic
— frank, tactless
— likes challenges
— independent, confident

— fun-loving, amiable
— hates commands, confinement
— leaps before looking
— tends to exaggerate

FLASH — the caring, loyal fireball. 19–22

— intense, emotional
— cool composure
— jealous, suspicious
— secretive

— hot-tempered
— caring and dedicated
— unforgiving, resentful
— determined, persevering

WOE — the sensitive, many-mooded worrier. 23–26

— active imagination
— unduly sensitive
— cautious, gentle
— prone to self-pity, worry

— artistic
— changeable moods
— insecure, touchy, fretful
— softhearted, protective

(Do not overlook the traits appearing after the name of the bird.)

PRANCE — the magnanimous, capable, proud ego 27–30

___ vivacious charm
___ condescending, pompous
___ responsible
___ loves praise

___ feels superior
___ opinionated, intolerant
___ good organizer, energetic
___ flair for showmanship

PONDER — the creative, compassionate dreamer 35–38

___ views world through
rose-colored glasses
___ helpful to others
___ noncompetitive
___ impractical, vague

___ slow-moving, lacks
purpose, discipline
___ sympathetic listener
___ humble, loves beauty
___ kind, sentimental

JETT — the ingenious, dynamic doer 39–42

___ busy, quick-acting
___ competitive, purposeful
___ belittles others
___ logical, resourceful

___ unpredictable
___ blunt, direct
___ aloof, innate coolness
___ keeps up-to-date

STEDDY — the patient, reliable, solid citizen 43–46

___ easy-going, steady
___ cautious, careful
___ procrastinates
___ tolerant, calm

___ stubborn
___ inflexible, resists change
___ self-indulgent, possessive
___ sensible, practical

PLUME — the modest, meticulous charmer 47–50

___ charming, joyful spirit
___ finicky, hard to please
___ sulks when criticized
___ sensitive, discriminating

___ warm, loving
___ neat, fastidious
___ corrects others
___ a perfectionist

BOOM — the impulsive, independent, big boss. 55–58

— great drive, enthusiasm
— bossy, takes charge
— quick-tempered
— set opinions

— "my way" self-centeredness
— venturesome, enterprising
— visionary, courageous
— open and direct

RIPPLE — the diplomatic, happy talker. 59–62

— talkative
— cheerful, agreeable
— gullible, naive
— strong sense of justice

— loves harmony
— changes mind, indecisive
— good sense of humor
— diplomatic, a peacemaker

EMBER — the shy, disciplined achiever. 63–66

— ambitious, goal-oriented
— low-keyed confidence
— broods when criticized
— poor mixer socially

— stern and strict
— determined, tenacious
— over-serious, duty-bound
— devoted to family

YAZOO — the inventive, absentminded rebel. 67–70

— analytical, curious
— unemotional nature
— idealistic, progressive
— friendly and loyal

— independent
— different, maybe eccentric
— a humanitarian
— perverse, rebellious

CONVERSATIONS:

Talk about specialness. 32
Understanding others better. 52
Shining up your specialness. 72
Good-bye. 76

Birds are special too. 78

Index. 79

About the author. 82

81

About the author

After 30-plus years of dealing with people, the author decided to capture their essence in still life, so to speak. The result—fanciful birds portraying our classic personalities.

The author's entire career has been in communications—radio, TV, magazines, newspapers. Born in Iowa, educated in Missouri (Lindenwood College) and Iowa (Drake University), she hop-scotched through jobs in Iowa, South Dakota, Colorado and Minnesota. But greener fields kept beckoning, so it was on to Chicago, then New York City.

After a ten-year career in the Big Apple, marriage prompted a move to Fairfield County, Connecticut. There she helped found and build a chain of weekly newspapers to a multi-million dollar status. She resigned to become an author and book publisher.

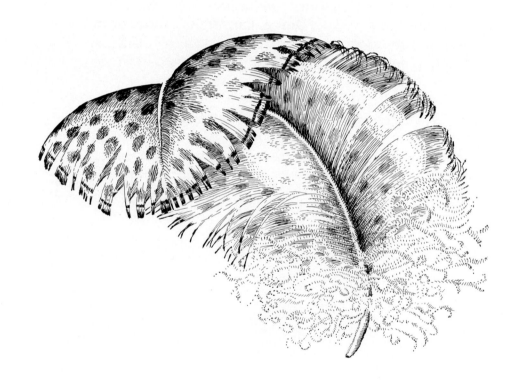